Melitta®

one:one™ cookbook

java shakes to tea cakes:

drink & dessert recipes

to enhance your

one:one™ experience

 Pascoe Publishing, Inc., Rocklin, California

Melitta one:one™ cookbook

ISBN: 1-929862-39-3

 Pascoe Publishing, Inc.
Rocklin, CA 95765
www.pascoepublishing.com

04   05   06   07   10   9   8   7   6   5   4   3   2   1

All books printed in China

one:one™ table of contents

pod

+

h₂o

ultimate
coffee
or tea

one:one™

introduction

Ever wonder why foods taste so incredibly delicious when paired with coffee or tea? Scones, muffins, biscotti, crème brûlée — the list goes on and on! The dark essence of coffee complements just about any other flavor and the clear purity of tea enhances flavors without overwhelming them. It's no surprise that specialty coffee and tea drinks are amazingly popular!

We've created exciting new recipes in this cookbook that will help you enjoy your Melitta® One:One™ Java-Pod™ Coffee Maker to the limit. Specialty coffee drinks such as *Iced Crème de Cacao, Caffè di Miele* and *Almond French Kiss Freeze* are easy to prepare, but carry wonderfully sophisticated delight. An experienced barista couldn't do better!

Specialty tea drinks are gaining popularity also. Check out our variety of tea recipes—healthful choices such as *Strawberry & Honey Breakfast Smoothie,* winter warmers such as *Coyote Cream Whisky,* and refreshingly cold teas, including a *Caribbean Rum Cooler.*

After you brew the perfect cup of coffee or tea in your Melitta® One:One™ Java-Pod™ Coffee Maker, sample the delectable recipes we've created as perfect partners for your drinks—*French Kisses™ Italian Tiramisu, Silky Chocolate Genoise with Raspberry Chocolate Glaze* and *Fresh Fruit Angel Meringue.* Keep your Melitta® One:One™ Java-Pod™ Coffee Maker on your counter and ready to go because everyone will be back for more!

one:one™ chapter one

gourmet coffee beverages

Creamy Caribbean Caffè

To prepare toasted coconut, spread the coconut on a small baking sheet. Preheat a toaster oven or full-sized oven to 350°F. Bake, stirring occasionally, until the coconut is a light golden color, about 12 minutes. Set aside to cool slightly.

1 tablespoon coconut milk

2 tablespoons whipping cream

1 1/2 teaspoons sugar

1 Java-Pod™ Buzzworthy™ coffee

1 tablespoon coconut, shredded and toasted

In a 12-ounce mug, combine the coconut milk, cream and sugar. Stir well to blend.

Place the mug in the Melitta® One:One™ Java-Pod™ Coffee Maker and brew an 8-ounce cup of Buzzworthy™ coffee as directed in the owner's manual.

Sprinkle the toasted coconut over the top of the hot coffee drink.

SERVES 1.

pod
+

h₂o

ultimate
coffee
or tea

Italian Hazelnut Caffè

Don't skimp when it comes to pure vanilla extract. There are many "imitation vanilla" flavors, but pure vanilla extract offers intensity that can't be matched.

1 egg white
1/2 teaspoon pure vanilla extract
1 Java-Pod™ Go Hazelnuts™ coffee
2 tablespoons whipping cream

In a small, deep bowl, beat the egg white with an electric mixer at high speed until soft peaks form. Gently add the vanilla and continue to beat until stiff peaks are formed.

Spoon the egg white into an 8-ounce mug. Place the mug in the Melitta® One:One™ Java-Pod™ Coffee Maker and brew a 5-ounce cup of Go Hazelnuts™ coffee as directed in the owner's manual.

Use the Melitta® frother to whip the cream. Spoon a dollop of cream on top of the hot coffee.

SERVES 1.

Spicy Turkish Caffè

Star anise is the fruit of a small evergreen tree native to China. It can be used as a flavoring or used as a ground spice (aniseed).

1 **Java-Pod™ Love At First Sip™ coffee**

1 **teaspoon** sugar

1 **tablespoon** chocolate syrup

1/8 **teaspoon** ground aniseed

3 **whole cloves**

1 **cinnamon stick**

2 **tablespoons** whipping cream

   orange and lemon zest for garnish

Place a 12-ounce mug in the Melitta® One:One™ Java-Pod™ Coffee Maker and brew an 8-ounce cup of Love at First Sip™ coffeee as directed in the owner's manual.

Pour the coffee into a small saucepan and add the sugar, chocolate syrup, aniseed, cloves and cinnamon stick. Heat the coffee over medium heat until it begins to simmer. Strain the hot coffee back into the 12-ounce mug to remove the spices.

Use the Melitta® frother to whip the cream and spoon a dollop on top of the hot coffee. Sprinkle the orange and lemon zest over the cream.

SERVES 1.

pod
+
h₂o

ultimate
coffee
or tea

Iced Crème de Cacao

A cool, yet delightfully rich iced coffee.

1/4 cup nonfat milk

1 tablespoon sugar

1/8 teaspoon pure vanilla extract

2 teaspoons crème de cacao

1 Java-Pod™ Skip the Buzz™ coffee

ice

In a 10-ounce mug, combine the milk, sugar, vanilla and crème de cacao.

Place the mug in the Melitta® One:One™ Java-Pod™ Coffee Maker and brew a 5-ounce cup of Skip the Buzz™ coffee as directed in the owner's manual.

Fill a 10-ounce beverage glass with ice and pour the hot coffee drink over the ice. Serve immediately.

SERVES 1.

Java & Cognac Shake

Perfect for a special Sunday brunch.

2 Java-Pods™ A Café Kind of Day™ coffee
2 cups vanilla ice cream
2 shots cognac
2 tablespoons chocolate syrup
2 tablespoons caramel syrup
  chocolate syrup and caramel syrup for
  garnish

Brew two 8-ounce cups of A Café Kind of Day™ coffee in the Melitta® One:One™ Java-Pod™ Coffee Maker as directed in the owner's manual.

Refrigerate the coffee until cool. In a blender, combine the chilled coffee, ice cream, cognac, chocolate syrup and caramel syrup. Mix on high speed until smooth, about 1 minute.

Pour the coffee shake into two chilled beverage glasses and drizzle the chocolate and caramel syrups over each shake.

SERVES 2.

pod
+

h₂o

ultimate
coffee
or tea

Peppermint & Cream Caffè

Is this coffee or dessert? You have the pleasure of deciding.

1 **small** candy cane
1 **ounce** peppermint schnapps
1 **Java-Pod™** Love at First Sip™ coffee
2 **tablespoons** whipping cream

Place the candy cane in a self-sealing plastic bag. Remove the air from the bag and seal. Using a heavy rolling pin, crush the candy cane into fine pieces.

Lightly moisten the rim of an 8-ounce mug with water. Dip the rim into the crushed candy pieces. Pour the peppermint schnapps into the mug, avoiding the rim of the mug.

Place the mug in the Melitta® One:One™ Java-Pod™ Coffee Maker. Prepare a 5-ounce cup of Love at First Sip™ coffee as directed in the owner's manual.

Use the Melitta® frother to whip the cream. Spoon the whipped cream on top of the hot coffee.

Sprinkle any remaining candy pieces on top of the cream.

SERVES 1.

Caffè di Miele

Taste a little bit of Italy in this delicious drink.

```
2 tablespoons honey
1/4 cup low fat milk
1 Java-Pod™ Buzzworthy™ coffee
pinch ground cinnamon
```

Pour the honey and milk into a 12-ounce mug and stir to combine.

Place the mug in the Melitta® One:One™ Java-Pod™ Coffee Maker and prepare an 8-ounce cup of Buzzworthy™ coffee as directed in the owner's manual.

Stir the hot coffee drink well to dissolve the honey completely and sprinkle the cinnamon over the coffee drink.

SERVES 1.

pod
+
h₂o

ultimate
coffee
or tea

Creamy Maple Caffè

*True Vermont maple syrup adds that oh-so-special
touch to this inviting drink.*

2 tablespoons genuine Vermont maple syrup
1/2 cup heavy cream
1 Java-Pod™ Skip the Buzz™ coffee

In a small saucepan, combine the maple syrup and cream. Cook
on very low heat until the cream is warm. Pour the cream into a
12-ounce mug.

Place the mug in the Melitta® One:One™ Java-Pod™ Coffee
Maker and prepare an 8-ounce cup of Skip the Buzz™ coffee.

Stir the coffee drink to blend and serve immediately.

SERVES 1.

Tangy Lemon Cooler

A truly refreshing drink for a hot summer day.
Zest the lemon by finely grating only the lemon peel, not
the white bitter pith beneath the peel.

2 Java-Pods™ Love At First Sip™ coffee
1 cup lemon sherbet or gelato
2 teaspoons freshly squeezed lemon juice
2 teaspoons lemon zest
2 teaspoons sugar

Brew two 5-ounce cups of Love at First Sip™ coffee in the
Melitta® One:One™ Java-Pod™ Coffee Maker as directed in the
owner's manual.

Refrigerate the coffee until chilled. In a blender, combine the
chilled coffee, sherbet, lemon juice, lemon zest and sugar until
smooth. Pour into two chilled glasses and serve.

SERVES 2.

pod
+
h₂o

ultimate
coffee
or tea

Almond French Kiss Freeze

*Grab your favorite magazine, pull up a deck chair
and sip on this sweet freeze!*

1 Java–Pod™ French Kisses™ coffee
1/4 cup vanilla frozen yogurt
1 1/2 tablespoons half and half
1 tablespoon amaretto
1 teaspoon pure vanilla extract
1/2 teaspoon almond extract
   crushed ice

Brew an 8-ounce cup of French Kisses™ coffee in the Melitta®
One:One™ Java-Pod™ Coffee Maker as directed in the owner's
manual.

Refrigerate the coffee until it is chilled. In a blender, combine
the chilled coffee, frozen yogurt, half and half, amaretto, vanilla
and almond extracts until smooth.

Spoon the crushed ice into a chilled beverage glass to fill
halfway. Pour the Almond French Kiss Freeze over the ice and
serve immediately.

SERVES 1.

Buttered Praline Coffee

The word "praline" is used to describe sugar-coated, caramelized nuts. That enticing taste of browned sugar and butter flavors the syrup used here.

1 Java-Pod™ Skip the Buzz™ coffee

1 tablespoon heavy cream

1 1/2 teaspoons dark brown sugar

1 tablespoon butter

1 1/2 tablespoons praline syrup

Brew a 5-ounce cup of Skip the Buzz™ coffee in the Melitta® One:One™ Java-Pod™ Coffee Maker as directed in the owner's manual.

Combine the coffee, cream, brown sugar and the butter in a small saucepan over low heat. Simmer until the sugar is dissolved, stirring often.

Add the praline syrup, stir to blend, and serve warm.

SERVES 1.

pod
+
h₂o

ultimate
coffee
or tea

Jamaican Rum Buzz

Feel the buzz!

1 Java-Pod™ Buzzworthy™ coffee
1 tablespoon molasses
2 tablespoons dark rum
2 tablespoons whipping cream

Brew an 8-ounce cup of the Buzzworthy™ coffee in the Melitta®
One:One™ Java-Pod™ Coffee Maker as directed in the owner's
manual.

Combine the coffee and the molasses in a small saucepan
and heat over medium temperature until the molasses is
dissolved, stirring often.

Pour the rum into a 12-ounce mug and top with the hot
coffee and molasses.

Use the Melitta® frother to whip the cream and garnish the
coffee with the whipped cream.

SERVES 1.

Sweet Wine & Cinnamon Sipping Coffee

*For added flavor, spritz the coffee with a splash of
fresh orange juice just before serving.*

2 ounces sweet wine of your choice
(sauterne, white zinfandel, etc.)
2 teaspoons sugar
1 teaspoon fresh orange zest
pinch ground cinnamon
2 Java-Pods™ Love At First Sip™ coffee

Divide the sweet wine, sugar, orange zest and cinnamon between
two 10-ounce mugs.

Place one mug in the Melitta® One:One™ Java-Pod™ Coffee
Maker and brew an 8-ounce cup of Love at First Sip™ coffee as
directed in the owner's manual. Repeat with the second mug. Stir
well to blend and enjoy.

SERVES 2.

pod
+
h₂o

ultimate
coffee
or tea

Spiced Eggnog Latte

A holiday drink rich with creamy goodness.

1/4 cup prepared eggnog
1/2 teaspoon ground cinnamon
1 Java-Pod™ Skip the Buzz™ coffee
1/4 cup whole milk, frothed (you may
   substitute whipped cream if desired)
pinch ground nutmeg

In a small saucepan on medium heat, warm the eggnog and cinnamon until it just begins to steam. Pour the heated eggnog into a large 12-ounce mug.

Place the mug in the Melitta® One:One™ Java-Pod™ Coffee Maker. Brew a 5-ounce cup of Skip the Buzz™ coffee as directed in the owner's manual.

Use the Melitta® frother to froth the milk and top the coffee with the frothed milk as desired. Sprinkle the nutmeg over the milk and stir slightly to combine. Serve immediately.

SERVES 1.

Grasshopper Latte

*The distinctive flavor of crème de menthe makes
this a must-have winter drink.*

1/4 cup whole milk

1 ounce crème de menthe liqueur

1 tablespoon chocolate syrup

1 Java-Pod™ A Café Kind of Day™ coffee

chocolate syrup for garnish

*In a small saucepan over medium heat, warm the milk until it
just begins to steam.*

*Add the crème de menthe and the chocolate syrup to the
warm milk and stir to combine. Pour the warm milk into a large
12-ounce mug.*

*Place the mug in the Melitta® One:One™ Java-Pod™ Coffee
Maker. Brew a 5-ounce cup of A Café Kind of Day™ coffee as
directed in the owner's manual.*

Stir and garnish with a swirl of chocolate syrup.

SERVES 1.

pod

+

h₂o

ultimate
coffee
or tea

Arabian Almond Roast

An excellent ending for your next romantic evening meal.

2 scoops vanilla ice cream (about 1/2 cup
    ice cream per scoop)
1/4 cup almond liqueur
2 Java-Pods™ Love at First Sip™ coffee
pinch ground cinnamon
2 whole cinnamon sticks

Spoon one scoop of ice cream each into two large 12-ounce mugs. Pour the liqueur equally over the ice cream.

Place one mug in the Melitta® One:One™ Java-Pod™ Coffee Maker and brew a 5-ounce cup of Love at First Sip™ coffee as directed in the owner's manual. Repeat with the second mug.

Stir once and sprinkle each serving with the ground cinnamon. Place one cinnamon stick in each drink to garnish.

SERVES 2.

Chocolate on Chocolate Caffè

Create chocolate shavings by running a sharp-bladed vegetable peeler over one side of a small semisweet candy bar. Store any unused chocolate in a self-sealing plastic bag in the refrigerator for up to 3 months.

1 tablespoon chocolate syrup
1 Java-Pod™ Buzzworthy™ coffee
1 scoop chocolate fudge ice cream
1 tablespoon semisweet chocolate shavings

Spoon the chocolate syrup into a large 12-ounce mug.

Place the mug in the Melitta® One:One™ Java-Pod™ Coffee Maker and brew a 5-ounce cup of Buzzworthy™ coffee as directed in the owner's manual.

Carefully place the scoop of ice cream in the coffee, sprinkle with the chocolate shavings and serve.

SERVES 1.

pod
+
h₂o

ultimate
coffee
or tea

Rocky Road to the Limit

Share some rocky road decadence with your best friends.

2 cups rocky road ice cream
1 teaspoon pure vanilla extract
2 Java-Pods™ Go Hazelnuts™ coffee
1/4 cup miniature marshmallows
pinch sweetened cocoa for garnish

Place the ice cream in a blender and blend at high speed for 30 seconds. Add the vanilla extract and blend for 10 seconds. Place the blender jar in the freezer while you prepare the coffee.

Brew a 5-ounce cup of Go Hazelnuts™ coffee in the Melitta® One:One™ Java-Pod™ Coffee Maker as directed in the owner's manual. Repeat with a second brew.

Fill a serving pitcher halfway with ice cubes. Pour the mugs of prepared coffee over the ice and allow it to chill for 15 minutes.

To serve, pour the chilled coffee equally into four glasses. Gently spoon the ice cream over each serving of coffee. Stir each drink once and garnish with miniature marshmallows and sweetened cocoa.

SERVES 4.

Easy Iced Caramelita

A fresh cup of coffee laced with rich caramel.

1 Java-Pod™ French Kisses™ coffee
3 tablespoons caramel syrup, divided

Place an 8-ounce mug in the Melitta® One:One™ Java-Pod™ Coffee Maker and brew a 5-ounce cup of French Kisses™ coffee.

Add 2 tablespoons of the caramel syrup and stir to blend. Fill a large beverage glass with ice and pour the hot drink over the ice.

Drizzle 1 tablespoon of caramel syrup over the coffee and serve.

SERVES 1.

pod
+

h₂o

ultimate
coffee
or tea

one:one™ chapter two

gourmet
tea
beverages

East Indian Lemon Black Tea

The British style of serving tea with lemon comes to your own kitchen. Cut the lemon into paper-thin slices for an authentic garnish.

1/4 teaspoon fresh lemon zest, finely grated

1 teaspoon sugar

2 teaspoons fresh lemon juice

1/4 teaspoon pure vanilla extract

1/8 teaspoon almond extract

1 Java-Pod™ Zen in Black™ tea

1 thin slice fresh lemon

In an 8-ounce mug, place the lemon zest, sugar, lemon juice and the vanilla and almond extracts. Stir to blend.

Place the mug in the Melitta® One:One™ Java-Pod™ Coffee Maker and brew a 5-ounce cup of Zen in Black™ tea as directed in the owner's manual.

Stir well to blend, garnish with the slice of lemon and enjoy.

SERVES 1.

pod
+
h₂o

ultimate
coffee
or tea

Citrus & Spice Jade Tea

Citrus & Spice Jade Tea is the perfect complement after a simple meal of roasted chicken or fillet of sole.

1 teaspoon fresh lemon juice

1 teaspoon fresh orange juice

1 1/2 teaspoons sugar

pinch ground cinnamon

pinch ground cloves

1 Java-Pod™ Shades of Jade™ tea

Place the lemon juice, orange juice, sugar, cinnamon and cloves in an 8-ounce mug and stir to combine.

Place the mug in the Melitta® One:One™ Java-Pod™ Coffee Maker and brew a 5-ounce cup of Shades of Jade™ tea as directed in the owner's manual.

Stir well to blend and serve while hot.

SERVES 1.

Very Apple Butter Tea

A soothing, gentle tea—infused with apple flavors and kissed with cinnamon.

1 Java-Pod™ Shades of Jade™ tea
2 tablespoons apple juice
1 tablespoon apple butter
  cinnamon stick for garnish

In an 8-ounce mug, brew a 5-ounce cup of Shades of Jade™ tea in the Melitta® One:One™ Java-Pod™ Coffee Maker as directed in the owner's manual.

Add the apple juice and apple butter and stir well to blend. Garnish with the cinnamon stick.

SERVES 1.

pod
+
h₂o

ultimate
coffee
or tea

Black Velvet

Lush black tea with a shot of pineapple sweetness.

2 tablespoons fresh pineapple juice
1 teaspoon lemon juice
1 Java-Pod™ Zen in Black™ tea
1 pineapple-flavored candy stick

In an 8-ounce mug, combine the pineapple juice and the lemon juice and stir to blend.

Place the mug in the Melitta® One:One™ Java-Pod™ Coffee Maker and brew a 5-ounce cup of Zen in Black™ tea as directed in the owner's manual.

Stir well with the candy stick and enjoy.

SERVES 1.

Cran-RazzBerry Jazz

A perfect "garden party" iced tea, with deep-fruit colors and a hint of clover honey.

2 Java-Pods™ All That Razzberry™ tea
1/4 cup cranberry juice
3 tablespoons clover honey
   crushed ice

Brew one 5-ounce cup of All That Razzberry™ tea in the Melitta® One:One™ Java-Pod™ Coffee Maker as directed in the owner's manual. Repeat with a second 5-ounce cup.

Refrigerate the tea to cool. Combine the cooled tea, cranberry juice and honey and stir well to blend. Fill two 10-ounce beverage glasses with crushed ice and pour the cooled tea over the ice.

SERVES 2.

pod
+
h₂o

ultimate
coffee
or tea

Hammock Honey Tea

*The best place to enjoy this brew is in the hammock
on a lazy afternoon.*

2 tablespoons clover honey

2 Java-Pods™ Shades of Jade™ tea

1/4 cup orange-pineapple-strawberry juice
   ice cubes

2 large fresh strawberries, culled and
   rinsed

Spoon the honey into two 10-ounce mugs. Place one mug into the Melitta® One:One™ Java-Pod™ Coffee Maker and brew an 8-ounce cup of Shades of Jade™ tea as directed in the owner's manual. Stir and set aside to cool. Repeat with the second mug.

Fill two 12-ounce beverage glasses with ice cubes. Pour the juice equally into the glasses, add the tea and stir.

Split each strawberry almost in half and place one strawberry on the rim of each glass as a garnish.

SERVES 2.

Shades of Emerald & Jade

Soothing crème de menthe brings serenity to your tea.

1 Java-Pod™ Shades of Jade™ tea
1 1/2 teaspoons crème de menthe syrup
1 tablespoon freshly squeezed lime juice
    crushed ice
2 fresh mint leaves for garnish
1 lime, thinly sliced for garnish

*Brew an 8-ounce cup of Shades of Jade™ tea in the Melitta®
One:One™ Java-Pod™ Coffee Maker as directed in the owner's
manual. Set aside to cool.*

*In a large beverage glass, combine the crème de menthe
syrup and lime juice and stir well. Add the cooled tea and stir
to blend.*

*Carefully add crushed ice and garnish with mint leaves and a
slice of lime.*

SERVES 1.

pod
+

h₂o

ultimate
coffee
or tea

Strawberry & Honey Breakfast Smoothie

This healthful smoothie will brighten up your morning. Add a tablespoon of soy powder, protein powder or half of a small banana before blending, if desired.

1 Java-Pod™ Shades of Jade™ tea

1/4 cup nonfat strawberry yogurt

2 tablespoons clover honey

1/4 cup frozen strawberries, sliced

whole fresh strawberries for garnish

Brew one 8-ounce mug of the Shades of Jade™ tea in the Melitta® One:One™ Java-Pod™ Coffee Maker as directed in the owner's manual. Refrigerate until cool.

In a blender, combine the cooled tea, yogurt, honey and the frozen strawberries.

Blend until smooth and pour into a large beverage glass. Garnish with fresh strawberries.

MAKES 1 SMOOTHIE.

Caribbean Rum Cooler

Ahoy! Sail away with this inviting drink.

2 Java-Pods™ Zen in Black™ tea
1/4 cup spiced dark or light rum
2 teaspoons fresh lemon juice
  crushed ice
  lemon peel for garnish

Brew one 8-ounce mug of Zen in Black™ tea in the Melitta®
One:One™ Java-Pod™ Coffee Maker as directed in the owner's
manual. Repeat with the second mug. Refrigerate until cool.

In two large beverage glasses, equally combine the rum and
lemon juice. Add the cooled tea to each glass and mix well.
Carefully add ice to the coolers and top each with a twist of
lemon peel.

SERVES 2.

pod
+
h₂o

ultimate
coffee
or tea

Coyote Cream Whiskey

When a pounding rain follows you home, it's time for
Coyote Cream Whiskey.

4 ounces whisky

2 tablespoons heavy cream

4 teaspoons sugar

2 Java-Pods™ Zen in Black™ tea

  whipped cream for garnish

In two 12-ounce mugs, equally combine the whisky, cream and
sugar and mix well.

  Place one mug in the Melitta® One:One™ Java-Pod™ Coffee
Maker and brew an 8-ounce cup of Zen in Black™ tea as
directed in the owner's manual. Repeat with the second mug.

  Stir well to combine and garnish each drink with a dollop of
whipped cream.

SERVES 2.

Black and White Chai Tea

A sophisticated tea to serve after that special dinner.

2 **teaspoons** vanilla extract

2 **tablespoons** chocolate sauce

1/2 **teaspoon** ground cinnamon

1/2 **cup** milk

2 **Java-Pods™** Chai tea

    whipped cream and cocoa powder for garnish

In two 10-ounce mugs, evenly divide the vanilla, chocolate sauce, ground cinnamon and milk. Stir to mix well.

Place one mug in the Melitta® One:One™ Java-Pod™ Coffee Maker and brew an 8-ounce cup of Chai tea. Stir to combine the flavors. Repeat with the second mug.

Top both drinks with a dollop of whipped cream and a dusting of cocoa powder.

SERVES 2.

pod
+
h₂o

ultimate
coffee
or tea

Ginger and Lime Chai Tea

This is a refreshing iced tea with subtle flavor nuances.

1 Java-Pod™ Chai tea
1/4 cup cream
1 teaspoon sugar
1/8 teaspoon ground cloves
1 thin slice ginger
   ice
1 lime slice for garnish

Brew an 8-ounce cup of Chai tea in the Melitta® One:One™ Java-Pod™ Coffee Maker as directed in the owner's manual. Set the tea aside to cool.

In a 16-ounce beverage glass combine the cream, sugar and cloves. Stir well to combine. Add the cooled tea and ginger slice and stir to blend. Carefully fill the glass with ice and garnish with a slice of lime.

SERVES 1.

Almond Roca Chai

A dessert drink at its best!

1 Java-Pod™ Chai tea
2 teaspoons caramel sauce
1 teaspoon almond extract
2 teaspoons chocolate sauce
1/4 cup cream
   ice
   almonds, thinly sliced for garnish

In a 10-ounce mug, brew an 8-ounce cup of Chai tea in the Melitta® One:One™ Java-Pod™ Coffee Maker as directed in the owner's manual.

Add the caramel sauce, almond extract and chocolate sauce to the hot tea and stir well to blend. Set aside to cool.

Pour the cream into a large beverage glass and carefully fill the glass with ice. Stir in the cooled tea to blend well. Garnish the dessert tea with almond slices.

SERVES 1.

pod
+

h₂o

ultimate
coffee
or tea

Cinnamon and Peppercorn Spice Chai

The peppercorns add just a subtle hint of spice.

1 Java-Pod™ Chai tea

1/8 teaspoon ground cardamom

1 cinnamon stick

2 peppercorns

1 teaspoon sugar

1/4 cup milk

frothed milk and ground cinnamon for garnish

In a 10-ounce mug, brew an 8-ounce cup of Chai tea in the Melitta® One:One™ Java-Pod™ Coffee Maker as directed in the owner's manual.

Stir in the cardamom, cinnamon stick and peppercorns. Add the sugar and milk and stir. Remove the peppercorns.

Top the hot spiced tea with frothed milk and a sprinkle of cinnamon. Serve with the cinnamon stick.

SERVES 1.

pod

+

h$_2$o

_____

ultimate
coffee
or tea

one:one™ chapter three

delicious ways
with your
coffee & tea

Cranberry Nut Biscotti

Spices, pistachios and almonds add to the fruit-laced biscotti.

3 cups all-purpose flour

1 cup sugar

1 teaspoon baking powder

1/2 teaspoon ground cinnamon

1/2 teaspoon ground allspice

2 eggs

1 tablespoon almond extract

1/2 cup pistachios, finely chopped

1/2 cup almonds, finely chopped

1 cup dried cranberries

pod

+

h_2o

ultimate
coffee
or tea

In a large bowl, combine the flour, sugar, baking powder, cinnamon and allspice. In a separate small bowl, whisk together the eggs and almond extract. Stir the eggs into the dry ingredients and add the nuts and cranberries. Blend well.

With floured hands, divide the dough evenly into 4 loaves and cover with a clean cloth. On a floured work surface, shape each loaf, one at a time, into a 1 1/2-inch-wide log. Place the logs on a baking sheet covered with parchment paper.

Bake in a 350°F oven for 30 minutes, until firm. Place the logs on a cooling rack and cool thoroughly.

With a serrated knife, cut the cooled biscotti into 1/2-inch slices. Place the biscotti, cut side up, on the baking sheet again. Bake for an additional 15 minutes. Place the baked biscotti on wire racks to cool. Store in an airtight container.

SERVES 8.

Warm Chocolate & Coffee Crème

Use this decadent and rich coffee crème as a complement to ice cream, fresh fruit or a simple cake. Or, add a few spoonfuls of crème to rich vanilla ice cream and blend to make an old-fashioned milk shake.

1 Java-Pod™ French Kisses™ coffee

1/2 cup heavy cream

1 teaspoon pure vanilla extract

1 cup prepared marshmallow crème

2 2-ounce semisweet baking chocolate bars, broken into pieces

Brew the French Kisses™ coffee in the Melitta® One:One™ Java-Pod™ Coffee Maker as directed in the owner's manual.

Place 2 teaspoons of the prepared coffee in a medium saucepan. Add the cream and the vanilla extract and cook over medium heat until warm, stirring often. Add the marshmallow crème and the baking chocolate and stir again.

Continue heating over low heat, stirring frequently, until the chocolate is melted and the sauce is smooth. Serve immediately or store in an airtight container in the refrigerator until ready to use.

MAKES 2 CUPS.

pod
+

h₂o

ultimate
coffee
or tea

Duo Caffè Layered Parfaits

This very delicious dessert is quite simple to prepare and it makes a lovely presentation at the table.

1 Java-Pod™ Love at First Sip™ coffee
2 1/2 cups whole milk, divided
1 2.5 ounce pkg. milk chocolate instant pudding
1 2.5 ounce pkg. dark chocolate instant pudding
1 cup freshly whipped cream semisweet chocolate curls

Brew an 8-ounce cup of Love at First Sip™ coffee in the Melitta® One:One™ Java-Pod™ Coffee Maker following the directions in the owner's manual. Refrigerate until chilled.

In a chilled medium mixing bowl, combine 2 cups of the milk with the milk chocolate pudding. Whisk together completely for 2 minutes. In a separate chilled bowl, add the remaining milk and the chilled coffee to the dark chocolate pudding mix and whisk for 2 minutes.

Using 4 parfait glasses, evenly spoon the dark chocolate pudding into each glass. Layer the milk chocolate pudding over the dark chocolate pudding in each glass. Top the milk chocolate pudding with a dollop of whipped cream and sprinkle with chocolate curls. Refrigerate or serve immediately.

SERVES 4.

Lemon-Iced Blueberry Tea Muffins

Rich and inviting with a tangy lemon frosting.

1 3/4 cups all-purpose flour

1/4 cup sugar

2 1/2 teaspoons baking powder

1 teaspoon salt

1 egg, beaten

3/4 cup nonfat milk

1/3 cup canola oil

1 cup fresh blueberries, rinsed and drained
(you may substitute frozen, thawed and
drained blueberries, if desired)

Tangy Lemon Frosting:

1 cup Neufchatel cheese, softened

2 tablespoons fresh lemon juice

2 teaspoons lemon zest

1 tablespoon powdered sugar

pod

+

h₂o

ultimate
coffee
or tea

Lightly coat a 12-cup muffin tin with cooking spray or shortening and preheat the oven to 400°F.

In a large mixing bowl, combine the flour, sugar, baking powder and salt and stir to blend well. In a small bowl, whisk together the egg, milk and oil. Add the liquid ingredients to the dry ingredients, whisking only until the dry ingredients are moistened. Do not over mix. Using a large rubber spatula, gently fold in the blueberries.

Fill the muffin cups two-thirds full with the batter. Bake for 25 minutes, or until a toothpick inserted in the middle of a muffin comes out clean.

Place the baked muffins on a cooling rack and cool before frosting.

To prepare the frosting, combine the cheese, lemon juice, lemon zest and powdered sugar together in a small bowl and whip until thoroughly blended. Frost the cooled muffins. Store any leftover muffins in an airtight container.

SERVES 12.

Shortbread Bites with Bittersweet Chocolate Glaze

Cookies so drenched in chocolaty flavor beg for a cup of hot coffee for balance. The perfect partner for these shortbread bites is Love at First Sip™ coffee.

1 cup butter, softened
1 cup sugar
2 eggs
1 1/4 cups all-purpose flour
2 tablespoons fresh lemon juice
1/2 teaspoon almond extract
1 teaspoon pure vanilla extract

Bittersweet Chocolate Glaze:

1/2 cup bittersweet chocolate chips
1 tablespoon butter

pod
+
h₂o

ultimate
coffee
or tea

In a large mixing bowl, beat the butter and sugar with an electric mixer until light and fluffy, about 3 minutes. Scrape the bowl often.

Add the eggs and mix at high speed again for 2 minutes to blend. Gently stir in the flour, lemon juice, almond extract and vanilla. Mix for 1 minute to incorporate the ingredients.

Preheat the oven to 300°F. Press the dough into an ungreased 9-inch x 13-inch baking pan. Using a sharp knife, score the dough into squares, 10 across horizontally and 8 across vertically.

Bake for 25 to 30 minutes, until lightly golden brown. Do not over bake the shortbread. Using a sharp knife, immediately cut through the previous scoring to separate the bars.

To glaze the shortbread, place the chocolate chips and the butter in a sealable plastic bag and close tightly. Place the bag in a bowl of hot, but not boiling, water. Knead the bag until the chocolate and butter are melted. Snip a very small opening in the corner of the bag and pipe a thin swirl of the glaze on top of each square.

MAKES 80 SHORTBREAD BITES.

Winter Persimmon & Golden Raisin Cookies

Brew a cup of French Kisses™ coffee to enjoy with these moist, inviting cookies.

4 persimmons, ripened

1 teaspoon baking soda

1 cup butter or margarine, softened

1 cup sugar

1 egg, beaten

2 cups all-purpose flour

1/2 cup golden raisins, finely chopped

1/2 cup walnuts, finely chopped

In a medium bowl, stir together the pulp of the 4 ripe persimmons and the baking soda and set aside.

In a large mixing bowl, cream the butter and sugar. Add the egg and persimmon pulp and mix well. Add the flour and combine thoroughly. Stir in the raisins and walnuts.

Preheat the oven to 350°F. Place small spoonfuls of cookie dough on a cookie sheet and bake for 10 to 15 minutes, until lightly browned. Place the baked cookies on a cookie rack to cool. Repeat with the remaining cookie dough. Store in an airtight container.

MAKES 3 DOZEN.

pod
+

h₂o

ultimate
coffee
or tea

Blackberry Buttermilk Loaf Cake

Cut generous slices for a country breakfast or brunch and serve with steaming cups of A Café Kind of Day™ coffee.

1 egg

1 cup lowfat buttermilk

1/4 cup vegetable oil

1 1/4 cups all-purpose flour

1 tablespoon baking powder

1/2 cup sugar

1 cup fresh blackberries
   (you may substitute frozen, thawed and drained blackberries)

In a small bowl, combine the egg, buttermilk and oil and whisk well. Set aside.

In a large mixing bowl, combine the flour, baking powder and sugar, stirring with a fork to incorporate. Make a well in the middle of the dry ingredients and add the egg mixture, stirring quickly. Gently fold in the blackberries.

Preheat the oven to 400°F. Lightly coat a 9-inch x 5-inch loaf pan with cooking spray or shortening. Spoon the batter into the prepared pan. Bake for 25 to 30 minutes.

The cake will be golden brown and firm in the middle when done. Transfer the cake to a wire rack and cool or serve warm.

SERVES 8.

European Sweet Cinnamon Bread

Enjoy the warm scent of fresh-baked sweet bread to start your day.

2 1/2 teaspoons dry yeast
1/2 cup warm cream, 105°F to 115°F
3 eggs, beaten, divided
1 cup sugar, divided
3 cups all-purpose flour
1/4 cup butter or margarine, softened
pinch salt
1 tablespoon lemon zest
1 tablespoon ground cinnamon

pod
+

h₂o

ultimate
coffee
or tea

Stir the yeast into the warm cream to dissolve. Set aside. In a small bowl, set aside 2 tablespoons of the beaten egg. In a separate small bowl, set aside 1 tablespoon of the sugar. In a large bowl, combine the flour, butter, remaining eggs and sugar, salt, zest and the warm yeast sponge.

Knead the dough for 7 minutes until soft and pliable on a floured surface. Lightly flour the dough and cover. Let it rise in a warm location for about an hour, or until doubled in size. Punch down the dough. Lightly coat a 9-inch x 5-inch loaf pan with cooking spray or shortening and place the dough in the prepared loaf pan.

Preheat the oven to 350°F. With a sharp knife, lightly cut across the top of the loaf lengthwise to make an indentation and brush lightly with the reserved egg. Combine the reserved sugar with the cinnamon and sprinkle generously over the top of the loaf.

Bake for 60 minutes or until a toothpick inserted in the center of the loaf comes out clean. Remove the pan from the oven and cool on a wire rack for 10 minutes. Turn the loaf out of the pan to cool completely.

SERVES 8.

Country Strawberry Scones

Scones probably originated in Scotland, where it is said that country cooks used oats as the main ingredient and cooked the scone batter, shaped into a round, on a griddle over the fire. The scones were then cut into triangles after cooking.

3 cups all-purpose flour

1/2 cup sugar

2 1/2 teaspoons baking powder

1/2 teaspoon baking soda

3/4 cup butter, chilled and cut into small pieces

1 cup buttermilk

2 teaspoons pure vanilla extract

1 cup fresh or frozen, thawed strawberries, sliced in half

2 tablespoons sugar

pod
+
h_2o

ultimate
coffee
or tea

Preheat the oven to 425°F. In a large bowl, sift together the flour, 1/2 cup sugar, baking powder and the baking soda. Cut the butter into the dry ingredients with a pastry cutter or two sharp knives just until the pastry is the size of small breadcrumbs.

In a small bowl stir together the buttermilk and the vanilla extract. Add the liquid ingredients to the dry ingredients using a fork. Mix just until the dough becomes sticky.

Turn the dough out onto a lightly floured board. With floured hands, knead the dough gently about a dozen times. Add the frozen or fresh strawberries during the last few turns and gently work them in.

Divide the dough in half. Pat each half into an 8-inch circle about 1/2-inch thick. Sprinkle each circle with 1 tablespoon of sugar. Press the sugar into the dough with the palm of your hand. With a long sharp knife, cut each round into 8 wedges. Place the wedges on an ungreased cookie sheet about 1/2-inch apart.

Bake for 15 to 18 minutes, or until the scones are golden. Remove the scones from the oven and cool about 5 minutes on the baking sheet before serving warm.

MAKES 16 SCONES.

Hot n' Saucy Barbeque Mop

Coffee is an excellent addition to many marinades and sauces. The coffee flavor balances and smoothes ingredients such as tomato sauce, mustard and vinegar. This sauce is excellent for grilled meats.

1 Java-Pod™ A Café Kind of Day™ coffee

12-ounce can tomato paste

1/2 cup water

1/2 cup prepared yellow mustard

1 tablespoon prepared horseradish

1/4 cup dark brown sugar

1/3 cup Worcestershire sauce

1 tablespoon butter

2 teaspoons ground black pepper

1 teaspoon garlic powder

1/2 teaspoon salt

1/4 teaspoon cayenne pepper

pod
+

h₂o

ultimate
coffee
or tea

Brew an 8-ounce cup of A Café Kind of Day™ coffee in the Melitta® One:One™ Java-Pod™ Coffee Maker as directed by the owner's manual. Refrigerate the coffee until cool.

In a large non-reactive saucepan, combine the cooled coffee, tomato paste, water, mustard, horseradish, brown sugar, Worcestershire sauce, butter, pepper, garlic powder, salt and cayenne pepper. Bring the sauce to a quick boil over high heat. Stir and blend well. Reduce the heat and simmer over very low heat, uncovered, for 10 to 15 minutes. Use immediately or refrigerate for up to 3 weeks in an airtight container.

MAKES ABOUT 3 CUPS.

Jamaican Citrus Marinade

Citrus juices, spices and coffee bring Jamaica to your grill! Try this marinade with skinless chicken breasts or lean pork medallions.

1 Java-Pod™ Love At First Sip™ coffee

5 cloves garlic, peeled

1/2 teaspoon salt

2 teaspoons dried oregano

1/2 teaspoon ground cumin

1/3 cup fresh orange juice

1/3 cup freshly squeezed lime juice

2 tablespoons vegetable oil

1/4 cup fresh parsley, minced

1/4 teaspoon ground black pepper

Brew an 8-ounce cup of Love At First Sip™ coffee in the Melitta® One:One™ Java-Pod™ Coffee Maker as directed in the owner's manual. Cool the coffee to room temperature.

Mash the garlic with the salt to make a paste. Scrape the garlic paste into a medium bowl and stir in the oregano and the cumin. Blend well. Whisk in the coffee, orange juice, lime juice, oil, parsley and black pepper until completely mixed. Use immediately or refrigerate for up to 2 days.

MAKES ABOUT 1 CUP.

pod

+

h₂o

ultimate
coffee
or tea

one:one™ chapter four

coffee bar &
dessert tray

Southern Belle Peanut Butter Pie

*Take the richness of cream cheese, peanut butter and ice cream
and add a jolt of coffee—perfect for any occasion!*

1 Java-Pod™ Buzzworthy™ coffee

3-ounce pkg. cream cheese, softened

1 cup powdered sugar

1/2 cup creamy peanut butter

1/4 cup whole milk

8-ounce container whipped topping

2 cups vanilla ice cream, slightly softened

Chocolate Cookie Pie Crust:

1 1/2 cups chocolate wafer cookie crumbs

1/4 cup sugar

1/2 cup butter, melted

pod
+
h₂o

ultimate
coffee
or tea

Prepare the pie crust by combining the cookie crumbs and the sugar in a medium bowl. Toss to mix well. Add the melted butter and stir. Press the crumbs firmly into a 9-inch pie plate. Cover and chill for at least 20 minutes until firm.

Brew an 8-ounce cup of Buzzworthy™ coffee in the Melitta® One:One™ Java-Pod™ Coffee Maker according to the directions in the owner's manual. Refrigerate the coffee to chill.

In a medium mixing bowl, beat the cream cheese with an electric mixer until light and fluffy. Add the sugar and peanut butter and beat well again, scraping the bowl often. Beat in the milk, adding it slowly to incorporate. Beat in the whipped topping and refrigerate for 30 minutes, or until chilled.

In a separate mixing bowl, use a flexible spatula to slowly blend the coffee into the ice cream. Mix until the coffee is thoroughly blended. Spread the coffee-flavored ice cream evenly over the piecrust. Spoon the cream cheese and peanut butter combination over the ice cream layer, mounding the pie in the center and smoothing it to the edges of the crust.

Cover the pie loosely with plastic wrap and freeze for 2 to 3 hours before serving.

SERVES 6 TO 8.

Caramel Crème Brûlée

This classic dessert is typically accompanied by a rich, full-bodied coffee. Serve with Love at First Sip™ coffee for pure delight.

6 large egg yolks

2 teaspoons pure vanilla extract

3 cups heavy cream

1/4 cup sugar

3 tablespoons caramel-flavored coffee syrup

6 tablespoons sugar, for garnish

Preheat the oven to 325°F. In a medium bowl, whisk together the egg yolks and the vanilla. Set aside. In a medium saucepan, heat the cream, 1/4 cup sugar and the caramel syrup over low heat, stirring occasionally. Do not allow the cream and sugar to get too warm or boil. As soon as the cream begins to steam and the sugar is dissolved, gradually whisk in the eggs, stirring constantly.

pod
+

h_2o

ultimate
coffee
or tea

Remove the crème brûlée from the heat. Butter six 4-ounce, oven-proof ramekins. Evenly divide the crème brûlée among the ramekins. Place the ramekins in a roasting pan. Place the pan in the oven and add enough water to the roasting pan to come halfway up the sides of the ramekins.

Bake the crème brûlée for about 1 hour. The custard should be barely set when done. To test, shake the custard. The center should jiggle slightly while the edges look set. Remove the ramekins from the water and place them on a wire rack to cool. Cover each ramekin and refrigerate for at least 4 hours. To serve, position the oven rack about 3 inches from the broiler. Preheat the broiler. Sprinkle the remaining 6 tablespoons of sugar evenly over each crème brûlée. Place the crème brûlée on a jellyroll pan under the broiler and heat until the sugar has melted and caramelized, about 2 minutes. Watch carefully to prevent the sugar from burning. Serve immediately or let the crème brûlée stand at room temperature for up to 1 hour.

SERVES 6.

Fresh Fruit Angel Meringue

Prepare this light, fruit-filled tart for your favorite guests.

1 9-inch refrigerated pie crust

1/2 cup water

1/2 cup sugar, divided

1 tablespoon cornstarch

5 large egg whites, at room temperature

1/4 teaspoon cream of tartar

1/8 teaspoon salt

1 1/2 cups fresh pears, peeled, cored and
   thinly sliced

1 1/2 cups fresh pineapple, peeled, cored
   and thinly sliced

Preheat the oven to 450°F. Fit the pie crust firmly into the bottom of a 9-inch tart pan with a removable rim. Bake until the crust is a light golden brown, 9 to 11 minutes. Remove the crust from the oven and cool.

pod
+
h₂o

ultimate
coffee
or tea

Combine the water, 2 tablespoons sugar and cornstarch in a small saucepan and blend well. Cook over medium-high heat, stirring constantly, until the liquid becomes clear, about 2 to 3 minutes. Remove from the heat and set aside.

Combine the egg whites, cream of tartar and salt in a medium, deep bowl and beat with an electric mixer at medium-high speed until frothy. Add the remaining sugar gradually to the egg whites, beating on high until soft peaks form, about 2 to 3 minutes. Do not allow the egg whites to become dry. Reduce the speed to medium and gradually add the clear cornstarch liquid, one spoonful at a time. Increase the mixer speed to high and beat until the meringue is smooth and satiny, about 2 minutes.

Arrange the pear slices over the pie crust, overlapping slices if necessary. Top the pear slices with the pineapple slices, arranging in the same manner. Spoon the meringue into a pastry bag fitted with a large star tip. Pipe the meringue on top of the arranged pears and pineapples to cover them completely.

Preheat the oven to 425°F. Bake the tart until the meringue is golden, 2 to 3 minutes. Watch carefully to avoid burning the meringue. Cool the tart completely on a wire rack. Run a small sharp knife between the rim and the crust to loosen it from the sides. Remove the rim. Cut the tart into wedges and serve.

SERVES 8.

Silky Chocolate Genoise with Raspberry Chocolate Glaze

*A dense and extremely smooth chocolate cake drenched
in raspberry glaze.*

12 ounces semisweet chocolate, chopped
1 cup unsalted butter, chilled and cut
  into pieces
6 large eggs, separated
3/4 cup sugar, divided
2 1/2 teaspoons pure vanilla extract

Raspberry Chocolate Glaze:

1/2 cup heavy whipping cream
1/2 cup dark corn syrup
9 ounces bittersweet chocolate, finely
  chopped
1 cup fresh raspberries, mashed (you may
  substitute frozen, thawed raspberries,
  if desired)

pod
+

h₂o

_____

ultimate
coffee
or tea

*Preheat the oven to 350°F. Butter a 9-inch springform pan and
line the bottom with a buttered sheet of parchment paper. Wrap
the outside of the pan with foil to seal completely.*

*In a heavy saucepan over low heat, melt the semisweet
chocolate and butter, stirring until smooth. Remove the pan from
the heat and cool to lukewarm, stirring often.*

*In a large bowl, beat the egg yolks and 6 tablespoons of sugar
with an electric mixer until the yolks are very thick and pale,*

about 3 minutes. Fold the melted chocolate and butter into the yolks and add the vanilla. Using clean, dry beaters, beat the egg whites in a medium, deep bowl until soft peaks form. Gradually add the remaining 6 tablespoons of sugar to the egg whites, beating until medium-firm peaks form.

Fold the egg whites into the chocolate batter in 3 batches. Pour the batter into the prepared springform pan and bake for 50 minutes. The top of the cake will be puffed and cracked and a toothpick inserted into the middle of the cake will have a few moist crumbs when the cake is done.

Place the cake on a wire rack to cool and gently press down on the top of the cake to flatten it evenly. Using a small knife, slide the blade between the rim of the pan and the sides of the cake to loosen. Let the cake cool and remove the pan rim. Place a sheet of waxed paper or foil under a cake rack and invert the cake onto the rack. Remove the parchment paper from the cake.

Prepare the glaze by combining the cream and the corn syrup in a medium saucepan. Heat to a simmer and remove from the heat. Add the chocolate and raspberries and whisk until melted. Carefully pour the glaze through a large strainer to remove the raspberry seeds.

Spread 1/2 cup of the glaze smoothly over the top and sides of the cake. Freeze the cake on the rack, uncovered, for about 3 minutes to set the glaze. Pour the remaining glaze over the cake and smooth the sides and top with a spatula. Chill the cake again until the glaze is firm.

SERVES 8

Tart Green Apple Cheesecake

Your guests will love the contrast between the tart green apples, smooth cheesecake and the crunchy apple crisp topping.

Crust:

1 cup all-purpose flour

3/4 cup rolled oats

1/2 cup dark brown sugar, packed

1 teaspoon ground cinnamon

1/2 cup butter or margarine, chilled

Cheesecake Filling:

8-ounce pkg. cream cheese, softened

1/2 cup sugar

1 egg

1 1/2 teaspoons pure vanilla extract

3 Granny Smith apples, peeled, cored and thinly sliced

1/2 cup almonds, chopped

pod
+
h₂o

ultimate
coffee
or tea

Preheat the oven to 350°F. In a medium bowl, combine the flour, oats, brown sugar and cinnamon, stirring to blend well. Cut in the butter with two knives or a pastry cutter until the mixture is uniformly the size of coarse crumbs. Lightly coat a 9-inch pie pan with cooking spray or shortening. Press two-thirds of the crust into the bottom of the prepared pan and set aside the remaining one-third. Bake the crust for 15 minutes until lightly browned.

In a medium bowl, beat the cream cheese with the sugar, egg and vanilla until very smooth. Spread the batter over the top of the baked crust. Arrange the sliced apples in concentric circles, overlapping slices if necessary. Sprinkle the apples with the remaining oat and sugar crust and top with the almonds. Place the cheesecake in the oven and bake for 30 minutes. Remove the cheesecake from the oven and cool on a wire rack.

Cover the cooled cheesecake and refrigerate for at least 2 hours before cutting into wedges.

SERVES 12.

Go Hazelnuts™ Chocolate Éclairs

Although these éclairs require some preparation and a bit of time to assemble, the effort is well worth the rewards!

Éclairs:

1 Java-Pod™ Go Hazelnuts™ coffee
1/2 cup butter or margarine
1 cup all-purpose flour, sifted
1/2 teaspoon salt
4 eggs

Custard Filling:

1/2 cup sugar
1/2 teaspoon salt
6 tablespoons all-purpose flour
2 cups whole milk
2 eggs, lightly beaten
2 teaspoons pure vanilla extract

Coffee Chocolate Glaze:

pod

+

h₂o

ultimate
coffee
or tea

1 Java-Pod™ Go Hazelnuts™ coffee
2 tablespoons shortening
2 ounces unsweetened chocolate
1 cup powdered sugar

Preheat the oven to 425°F. Brew an 8-ounce cup of Go Hazelnuts™ coffee in the Melitta® One:One™ Java-Pod™ Coffee Maker as directed in the owner's manual.

In a medium saucepan, bring the butter and the coffee to a quick boil. Add the flour and salt. Cook over medium heat, stirring constantly until the dough forms a ball and leaves the sides of the pan. Remove the pan from the heat. Add the eggs, one at a time, beating vigorously after each addition so that the dough is smooth and glossy.

Drop the dough by tablespoons 3 to 4 inches apart on an ungreased cookie sheet to form 12 puffs. Bake for 30 to 35 minutes, or until the puffs are golden brown. Turn the oven off.

Slice the hot éclair puffs in half. Place the halves open on the cookie sheet and put them back into the oven for 20 minutes. Do not heat the oven. This allows the center of each éclair to dry. Remove the éclairs from the oven and cool on wire racks.

To prepare the custard, measure the sugar, salt and the flour into a medium saucepan. Whisk in the milk until smooth and cook over low heat. Stir constantly until the milk boils. Boil 1 minute and remove from the heat.

In a small bowl, lightly beat the eggs. Whisk a little of the hot milk into the eggs. Whisk the eggs and milk back into the saucepan. Cook over medium heat, bringing the custard to a boil again. Stir constantly to avoid burning. Remove from the heat, cool and add the vanilla. Set aside.

To prepare the glaze, brew a 5-ounce cup of Go Hazelnuts™ coffee in the Melitta® One:One™ Java Pod™ Coffee Maker

continued pg. 70

Go Hazelnuts™ **Chocolate Éclairs** *continued from pg. 69*

according to the owner's manual. Melt the shortening and the chocolate together in a small saucepan, stirring until smooth. Transfer the chocolate to a large bowl and add the powdered sugar and 2 tablespoons of the freshly brewed coffee. Beat with an electric mixer on high speed until smooth. You may add a small amount of coffee if needed for the desired consistency.

To assemble, fill one éclair half with one heaping tablespoon of custard. Cover with the remaining éclair half and drizzle with the glaze. Repeat with the remaining éclairs. Serve immediately or refrigerate in an airtight container in the refrigerator.

SERVES 12.

pod
+
h₂o

ultimate
coffee
or tea

Midnight Sky Chocolate Pie

A new, delectable twist on pecan pie.

3 eggs

1 cup dark corn syrup

2/3 cup sugar

3 tablespoons butter, melted

1 1/2 teaspoons pure vanilla extract

2 cups Brazil nuts, finely chopped

1/2 cup semisweet chocolate morsels

1 9 to 10-inch pie crust, unbaked

Preheat the oven to 350°F. In a large bowl, combine the eggs, corn syrup, sugar, butter and vanilla extract. Beat with an electric mixer for 2 minutes, or until thoroughly blended. Fold in the Brazil nuts.

Spread the chocolate morsels over the pie crust in a single layer. Carefully pour the Brazil nut filling over the chocolate morsels and bake for 45 minutes, until the filling is set. Place the baked pie on a wire rack and cool completely before serving.

SERVES 8

French Kisses™ Italian Tiramisu

Tiramisu is a popular dessert of Italian origin. It traditionally includes ladyfingers soaked in coffee, zabaglione cream, mascarpone cheese and bitter chocolate. This recipe includes all of the important elements, including French Kisses™ coffee, for delicious results.

Custard:

8 large egg yolks

1/4 cup sugar

2 cups heavy whipping cream

2 1/2 teaspoons pure vanilla extract

12 lady fingers

Syrup:

1 Java-Pod™ French Kisses™ coffee

1/4 cup sugar

2 tablespoons water

1 teaspoon crème de cacao liqueur

Toppings:

1 cup mascarpone cheese, softened

1 tablespoon unsweetened cocoa powder

pod

+

h₂o

ultimate
coffee
or tea

Preheat the oven to 300°F. To make the custard, combine the egg yolks and sugar in a large bowl. Beat with an electric mixer on high speed until the batter is thickened and pale yellow, 4 to 5 minutes. Add the whipping cream and vanilla and beat just until mixed. Set aside.

Place 2 ladyfingers in the bottom of each of 6 buttered ramekins. Brew a 5-ounce cup of French Kisses™ coffee in the Melitta® One:One™ Java-Pod™ Coffee Maker according to the owner's manual. Combine the sugar, water, liqueur and 2 tablespoons of the coffee in a measuring cup and mix well. Pour the syrup evenly over the ladyfingers.

Divide and spoon the prepared custard evenly among the ramekins. Place the ramekins in a 9-inch x 13-inch baking pan. Place the pan with the ramekins on the center rack in the oven. Pour very hot water into the baking pan, filling the pan to within 1/2-inch from the top of the ramekins.

Bake the tiramisu until each is set around the edges, but still slightly soft in the center, 40 to 50 minutes. Remove the pan carefully from the oven and allow the tiramisu to stand in the water for about 2 hours, until the centers are set. Remove the ramekins to a cooling rack.

When the tiramisu is cooled, spread the mascarpone cheese over each and dust with the cocoa powder.

MAKES 6 SERVINGS.

Gelato di Caffè

Put a buzz in your own gelato!

1 Java-Pod™ Buzzworthy™ coffee
3/4 cup unsweetened cocoa powder
3/4 cup sugar
pinch salt
1/2 cup whole milk
2 eggs, well beaten
1 1/2 cups heavy whipping cream

Brew a 5-ounce cup of Buzzworthy™ coffee in the Melitta®
One:One™ Java-Pod™ Coffee Maker according to the owner's
manual and cool.

In a medium saucepan, whisk together the cocoa, sugar and
salt. Add the milk, 1/2 cup of coffee and the eggs. Whisk and
cook over medium heat, stirring constantly, until steaming hot
and starting to thicken. This may take 6 to 8 minutes. Stir
constantly as the milk and eggs heat. Whisk in the cream and
chill thoroughly, preferably 8-12 hours.

When ready to freeze, follow the owner's manual instructions
for your ice cream maker. You may also prepare the gelato by
freezing it for 3 hours, until firm around the edges. Scrape the
gelato into a blender and process on high speed for 10 seconds.
Return the gelato to the freezer and freeze until firm, about 3
hours. Blend again just prior to serving. The gelato will be very soft.

pod
+
h₂o

ultimate
coffee
or tea

MAKES ABOUT 1 QUART.

Baked Pears in Marsala

Prepare this easy dessert when Bartlett or Bosc pears are in season. Choose ripe pears that are slightly soft and unblemished.

4 pears, peeled and cut in half,
    cores removed
1/4 cup marsala wine
pinch ground nutmeg
pinch ground cloves
    sour cream for garnish

Arrange the pear halves, cut side down, in a microwave-safe glass pan. Splash each pear with the marsala wine and sprinkle the nutmeg and cloves over each pear.

Cover the pears with plastic wrap and microwave on High for 10 to 12 minutes, or until the pears are softened and hot throughout. To serve, plate the pears and pour the wine and spices from the pan over each. Garnish each serving with a small spoonful of sour cream.

Serves 4.

pod

+

h₂o

ultimate
coffee
or tea